MARIE CURIE

By Andrew Santella

WORLD ALMANAC® LIBRARY

JB.
Curie S

Please visit our web site at: www.worldalmanaclibrary.com
For a free color catalog describing World Almanac® Library's list of high-quality books
and multimedia programs, call 1-800-848-2928 (USA) or 1-800-461-9120 (Canada).
World Almanac® Library's Fax: (414) 332-3567.

Library of Congress Cataloging-in-Publication Data

Santella, Andrew.
  Marie Curie / by Andrew Santella.
    p. cm. — (Trailblazers of the modern world)
  Includes bibliographical references and index.
  Summary: Presents the life and accomplishments of the Polish-born chemist, discussing her discovery of radium
and the development of the use of X rays in medicine.
  ISBN 0-8368-5061-0 (lib. bdg.)
  ISBN 0-8368-5221-4 (softcover)
  1. Curie, Marie, 1867-1934—Juvenile literature. 2. Chemists—Poland—Biography—Juvenile literature.
  [1. Curie, Marie, 1867-1934. 2. Chemists. 3. Women—Biography.] I. Title. II. Series.
  QD22.C8S26   2001
  540'.92—dc21
  [B]   2001034177

This North American edition first published in 2001 by
World Almanac® Library
330 West Olive Street, Suite 100
Milwaukee, WI 53212 USA

This U.S. edition © 2001 by World Almanac® Library.

An Editorial Directions book
Editor: Lucia Raatma
Designer and page production: Ox and Company
Photo researcher: Dawn Friedman
Indexer: Timothy Griffin
Proofreader: Neal Durando
World Almanac® Library art direction: Karen Knutson
World Almanac® Library editor: Jacqueline Laks Gorman
World Almanac® Library production: Susan Ashley and Jessica L. Yanke

Photo credits: Corbis/Bettmann, cover, 4, 5; Hulton/Archive/Hulton Getty, 6; Hulton/Archive/Hulton Getty/Popperfoto,
7; Corbis/Massimo Listri, 8; Hulton/Archive/Hulton Getty, 9; Hulton/Archive/Hulton Getty/Popperfoto, 11;
Hulton/Archive/Hulton Getty, 13; Corbis/Gianni Dagli Orti, 14; Hulton/Archive/Hulton Getty/Scott Swanson Collection,
15; Hulton/Archive/Hulton Getty, 16; Hulton/Archive/Hulton Getty/Popperfoto, 17; Hulton/Archive/Agence France
Presse, 19; Hulton/Archive, 20; Hulton/Archive/Roger Viollet, 21; AP/Wide World Photos, 22 top, 22 bottom; AP/Wide
World Photos/American Institute of Physics, 23; Corbis/Bettmann, 24, 25, 26, 27; Hulton/Archive 28–29, 30;
Hulton/Archive/Hulton Getty, 31; Corbis/Roger Ressmeyer, 32; Hulton/Archive/Hulton Getty, 33, 34, 35, 36, 37, 38;
Corbis/Bettmann, 39; AP/Wide World Photos, 40–41; Hulton/Archive/Hulton Getty, 41 top, Hulton/Archive/Illustrated
London News, 42; Corbis/Bettman, 43.

Printed in the United States of America

1 2 3 4 5 6 7 8 9 05 04 03 02 01

30652001069329

TABLE of CONTENTS

CHAPTER 1   THE NEW WORLD OF SCIENCE   4

CHAPTER 2   EARLY LIFE   6

CHAPTER 3   ON TO PARIS   13

CHAPTER 4   BECOMING PARTNERS   19

CHAPTER 5   MAKING DISCOVERIES   26

CHAPTER 6   FINDING FAME   30

CHAPTER 7   WORK AND LOSS   34

            TIMELINE   44

            GLOSSARY   45

            TO FIND OUT MORE   46

            INDEX   47

THE NEW WORLD OF SCIENCE

Marie Curie's work helped change the world of science.

One day in 1897, a young woman living in Paris began a series of scientific experiments. She had just earned her college degree in **physics** and was working toward a more advanced degree. She had other things on her mind as well. Just three months earlier, she had given birth to her first child—a little girl named Irène. Each night, she hurried home from her experiments to give Irène a bath and put her to bed. The young woman's name was Marie Curie. Her experiments helped change the world of science forever.

Marie Curie in her laboratory

IMPORTANT EXPERIMENTS

At that time, few people could have guessed that Marie's experiments were so important. For one thing, she was working in a drafty, dusty shed, rather than in a new, well-equipped laboratory. The roof leaked and the walls were crumbling, but Marie was just starting her work as a scientist, and that shed was the best workplace she could afford.

In that shed, however, Marie Curie began the research that made her one of the world's most famous scientists. She won great honors in her field, including two **Nobel Prizes**—one in physics and one in **chemistry**—for the work she began there. She also became the first woman to teach at her university. Her discoveries led to a new age in medical research and new ways to treat diseases such as cancer.

SCIENTIFIC SACRIFICE

Marie Curie's discoveries helped generations of cancer patients, but they also made Marie very sick. For much of her life, she suffered from fevers, dizziness, and vision problems. Still, she did not let her illness keep her from the work she loved. "Nothing in life is to be feared," she later wrote. "It is only to be understood."

CHAPTER 2

EARLY LIFE

Warsaw, Poland, in the mid-1800s

arie Curie became famous for the work she did in Paris, but France was not her first home. She was born as Maria Sklodowska on November 7, 1867, in Warsaw, Poland. Maria was the youngest of five children, and both of her

Maria (left) with her father and two of her sisters in 1885

parents were educators. Her father taught math and physics while her mother, a musician, was **headmistress**, or principal, of a private school for girls.

LEARNING TO LOVE SCIENCE

Her parents passed on their love of learning to Maria and her siblings. Her father liked to read to the Sklodowska children at night. On special occasions, he even read them poems he had written. Maria's mother taught her songs about the history of Poland, and mother and daughter often sat at the piano together playing and singing these songs.

The family encountered difficulties when Maria was ten. Her mother died, and that same year her father lost his job. To help pay the bills, the family rented out rooms in their house to **boarders**, and Maria did her part by preparing breakfast for the boarders and doing other chores. Because the boarders used what had been her bedroom, she had to sleep on the living room floor.

Despite these hardships, Maria proved to be an exceptional student with an outstanding memory. By the time she was ten, her teachers were bragging about Maria to visiting school inspectors. The subject that seemed to interest Maria above all others was science. Her father kept scientific equipment in a glass case in the house. Even as a little girl, Maria was fascinated by these scientific instruments and what could be learned from them.

Maria graduated from high school when she was only fifteen years old—and

Young Maria was fascinated by her father's scientific instruments.

Poland

Poland had once been a powerful nation, but by the time Maria Sklodowska was born, Poland was no longer even a country. In the 1700s, parts of Poland had been taken over by Russia, Prussia, and Austria. The city of Warsaw was controlled by Russia. Polish patriots resisted Russian rule for years, but their efforts often led to even harsher measures imposed by Russia on Polish people. At that time, it was against the law to teach Polish history or the Polish language. Russian soldiers often stopped and searched Polish citizens at random (above).

As a result, Maria's memories of her school years were grim. "[We were] constantly held in suspicion and spied upon," she recalled. "The children knew that a single conversation in Polish . . . might seriously harm not only themselves, but also their families."

she earned top grades. Her success at school was remarkable because she was being taught in a foreign language. Russia ruled Poland when Maria was a girl, so the Russian language was used in Poland's schools. Maria grew up speaking Polish at home, but she had to speak Russian at school.

At her graduation, Maria was awarded a gold medal. She wanted to continue her education, but it was not easy for women in Poland to attend college in those days. In fact, the University of Warsaw did not admit women until thirty-two years later.

A PLAN FOR COLLEGE

Maria knew that if she wanted to continue her education, she would have to attend college outside of Poland. She also knew that she would have to earn money, so she began giving private lessons to children of wealthy parents in Warsaw. Her earnings helped the family get

Free Universities

Most Polish women were not allowed to attend college, but that doesn't mean they gave up trying to educate themselves. Some took part in illegal "free universities." These were groups of people who met in secret to help each other learn. They met at night in private homes, and because they met in different places, these groups were sometimes called "wandering universities." They listened to lectures, borrowed books, and taught one another. The goal of the free universities was to make the Polish people stronger through education.

by, but she knew she would need a lot more for college.
Her sister Bronya also wanted to continue in school,
and she hoped to study medicine. So Maria and Bronya
worked out a deal. Maria would find work to help pay
for Bronya's medical studies. Then, when Bronya was
working as a doctor, she would help pay for Maria's
studies.

Maria went to work as a **governess** for the Zorawski
family on a country **estate** located 60 miles (97 kilome-
ters) south of Warsaw. There she tutored two of the
Zorawski children, and she also tried to educate herself.
She rose early in the morning and studied before doing
her work. Late at night, she studied more. When she
grew tired of reading, she simply turned to another
activity. "When I feel myself quite unable to read . . .

I work on problems of algebra or trigonometry [a branch of mathematics]," she wrote in her journal.

Maria was working toward her goal of studying in Paris, where women were allowed to attend college. She decided that physics and mathematics would be her subjects. "I resolutely undertook a serious preparation for future work," she wrote.

A BROKEN HEART

Despite all her hard work, Maria managed to find time to fall in love. One summer, the Zorawskis' son Kazimierz came home on his break from college. Maria and Kazimierz fell in love and soon began planning to marry. When they told Kazimierz's parents about their plans, however, the Zorawskis objected. They didn't want their son to marry a governess—they had better things in mind for him.

Maria was heartbroken, but she continued tutoring at the Zorawski estate. After working there for three years, she returned to Warsaw and worked as a governess there for another year. Finally, in 1891, she and her sister decided it was time for Maria to begin her studies, and she began preparing to leave for Paris and her future work.

Maria chose Paris because she wanted to attend the great university there. The University of Paris—the **Sorbonne**—was home to some of Europe's greatest thinkers, and the science teachers at the Sorbonne were among the world's most **eminent** scientists. In Poland, Maria had not been allowed to attend the best schools. In Paris, she would have the chance to learn from the leading scholars of the time.

Maria a few months after arriving in Paris

The University of Paris

The University of Paris was founded in 1170 and is one of the world's oldest universities. The university is made up of several schools, each institution teaching different subjects. One of the most renowned of these schools is the Sorbonne, founded in 1201 by Robert of Sorbon, the chaplain of King Louis IX. Students at the original Sorbonne studied **theology** (the study of religion). The Sorbonne became so famous that its name is sometimes used for all the schools of the University of Paris.

LEAVING HOME

Maria did not want to leave her family or her own country, but the promise of Paris was too great to pass up. She said a tearful good-bye to her father and boarded a train for Paris, but the journey was far from easy. Maria had to ride in a crowded train carriage surrounded by luggage. She felt fortunate to be on her way to Paris, though. Many other young people had endured much greater hardship to get there. Paris attracted talented, bright people from all over Europe. They came from many different countries—by ship, by train, or even on foot.

When Maria arrived in Paris, she found one of the world's most exciting cities. The bookstores of Paris overflowed with new books, and students spent hours in stimulating discussions of fascinating ideas in cafés throughout the city. Unlike in Poland, people did not have to be afraid to speak their native language. Maria had never been anywhere quite like Paris. "A new world opened to me," she wrote, and on November 3, 1891, she enrolled at the Sorbonne.

Paris in 1891

Paris was a place of great excitement in 1891. That year, the first electric lights appeared in the city. Parisians also enjoyed a new landmark in the city. The Eiffel Tower (above), designed by an engineer named Gustave Eiffel, was completed in 1889 as a monument for the Universal Exposition of that year. At 984 feet (300 meters), it was the world's tallest structure.

AT THE SORBONNE

Maria embraced Paris. She worked hard to learn the French language and even changed her name to make it sound more French. When she registered at the Sorbonne, she signed her name "Marie." However, living in Paris was difficult for Marie. To begin with, very few women studied at the Sorbonne. Of 1,800 students there, only twenty-three were women. This was because although women were free to attend college in France, few actually did. France was a man's world in the late 1800s. Men held almost all the important positions in business, politics, and other fields, as well as at French universities. For example, all the teachers at the Sorbonne were men. A brilliant woman like Marie could enroll at the Sorbonne—but she would have to put up with many people who thought she did not belong there.

SERIOUS STUDIES

Marie was determined to succeed at the university, so she worked hard on her French, since all her classes were taught in that language. In addition, when she noticed

opposite: Paris was a busy and exciting place for Marie and other students.

Marie became the first woman to earn a physics degree from the Sorbonne.

The Curie Philosophy

Marie did not complain about her life, and she later explained:

*Life is not easy for any of us. But what of that? We must have **perseverance** and above all confidence in ourselves. We must believe that we are gifted for something and that this thing must be attained.*

how advanced other students were in their math skills, she worked hard to catch up on mathematics too. She studied so much that her sister Bronya worried about her.

At first, Marie lived with her sister. Bronya's house was not near the Sorbonne, however, and Marie spent an hour going to and from school each day. To save time, she moved to an apartment closer to school. It was just a small space in an attic, though, and she had to climb six flights of stairs to reach it! In the summer, it grew very warm under the slanted roof, and in the winter, cold winds blew through gaps in the wall. Also, the rent for that tiny apartment cut into Marie's **meager** savings. Some nights, she ate only a little French bread and some chocolate for dinner. Then she studied late into the night.

Bronya looked in on Marie now and then. Sometimes, she would make Marie take a break and come home with her for a decent meal. Marie never took a very long break, however. Very quickly, she would return home to her apartment and get back to work. Marie lived like this for two years. Finally, in 1893, she was ready to find out if all her work would pay off. She took an exam to get her degree in physics—a branch of science that studies natural laws—and Marie made history. Not only did she pass the exam, but she finished with the highest marks in her class. Marie was the first woman to earn a degree in physics from the Sorbonne.

Marie didn't spend all her time studying, though. She made friends with other Polish students and teachers at the university because she was seriously thinking about returning to Poland and getting a job as a teacher there. Then, one day when she was visiting one of her Polish friends, something happened that would change her life. She met a man named Pierre Curie.

ROMANCE

Pierre Curie was a scientist, born and raised in Paris. When he met Marie, he was already doing important scientific work there. Their first conversation was about science, and the two soon grew to like one another. They visited each other and talked about their work. Pierre started sending Marie long letters, and she would stop whatever she was doing to read them. Pierre and Marie began to see themselves as a team. Marie dropped her plans to return to Poland. Instead, she stayed in Paris and began a new life with Pierre.

On July 26, 1895, Marie and Pierre were married. Their small wedding was held in the city hall in Sceaux, France, and for the ceremony, Pierre and Marie wore their everyday clothes.

Marie and Pierre Curie were partners in marriage and in the laboratory.

Bicycles

When the Curies went on their first bike ride, bicycles had been around for only a few years. The first popular bicycle was invented by Pierre Michaux and his son Ernest in 1861. It was made of wood and iron, and it rattled so much that it was called the "boneshaker."

Some friends gave them two bicycles as a wedding gift, so the newlyweds spent their honeymoon riding their new bikes around the charming French countryside. Over the years, Marie and Pierre returned to the country often, riding their bikes together whenever they had the chance.

The newlyweds rented a small apartment in Paris. Pierre earned a modest salary as a college professor, while Marie continued her studies. In September 1897, Marie gave birth to a daughter whom the couple named Irène.

Wilhelm
Roentgen

The laboratory where
Roentgen did his work
with X rays

CHANGING SCIENCE

Marie Curie's life was changing, and so was the world of science. Scientists all over the world were making discoveries that transformed the way people lived.

In 1895—the year the Curies were married—a German scientist named Wilhelm Roentgen noticed something amazing. One day, during an experiment in his laboratory, Roentgen was working with a **Crookes tube**, an empty glass tube through which an electric current is passed. He covered the tube with black paper. When he turned on the electric current, he noticed that a dark image appeared on a photographic plate near the tube.

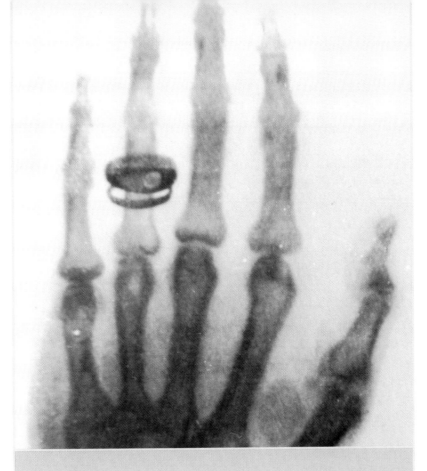

X rays

X rays are invisible, but they can be used to take a special kind of photograph. X-ray photographs can show the interior of some things, including the human body.

Wilhelm Roentgen was the first to demonstrate X-ray photography. At a lecture in 1896, he called another scientist onto the stage with him, and he took an X-ray photograph of the scientist's hand (above). When the photograph was developed, the audience could see the bones of the scientist's hand, fingers, and wrist. The amazed members of the audience jumped to their feet and applauded.

The use of X rays revolutionized medical and surgical techniques, and they eventually provided scientists with new insights into the nature of radiation as well as the structure of the atom. In Germany, X rays were called *Roentgen rays* in his honor.

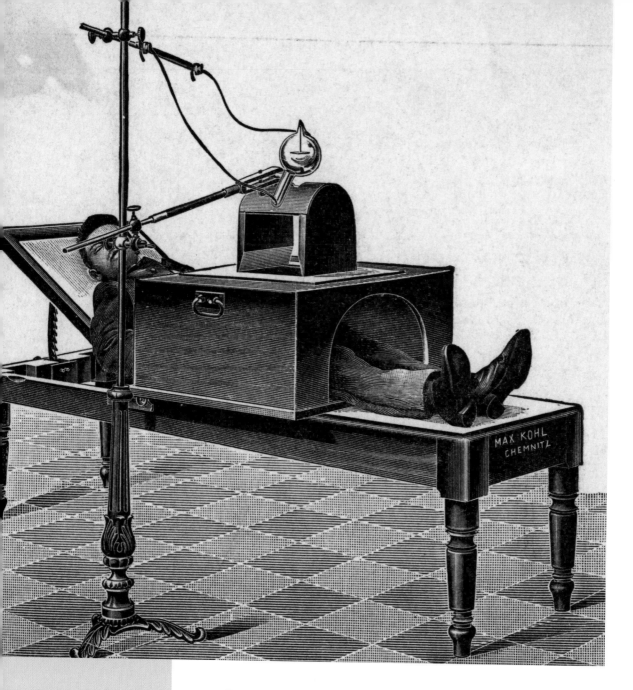

An early X-ray machine

Roentgen was fascinated by these unknown, invisible rays that were coming from the tube. These rays were a mystery to him, so he named them X rays.

He noticed that the X rays passed easily through some substances, such as skin, but were stopped by others, such as metal or bone. Because of this, Roentgen could photograph the bone structure of his wife's hand with the rays.

After Roentgen's discovery, people all over the world began experimenting with X rays. A scientist named Antoine Henri Becquerel found another kind of ray that was even more powerful than X rays. He was not able to learn much about these rays, however. Marie Curie was beginning her career as a scientist at that time, and she was interested in Becquerel's work. She wanted to know why certain substances radiated, or gave off rays, and she talked about it with Pierre and other scientists. She wanted to know what radiation was and where it came from.

Late in 1897, Marie Curie started her work. She began by trying to understand more about the radiation Becquerel had found, and she came up with a name for this kind of radiation. She called it **radioactivity.** Marie was the first person to use this word, and what she learned about radioactivity changed the world of science and medicine.

Antoine Henri Becquerel

CHAPTER 5

MAKING DISCOVERIES

Marie—and other scientists like her—knew that everything in nature was made up of **elements**. An element is a substance that can't be broken down into other substances. When Marie began her work, scientists thought they had found all the elements that existed, but they were wrong.

Marie Curie spent many long hours on her experiments.

Marie began testing different kinds of natural materials. One of the things she tested was a mineral called **pitchblende**. Scientists believed that pitchblende was made up chiefly of oxygen and uranium. However, Marie's tests showed that pitchblende was much more radioactive than those elements, giving off much stronger rays than those elements did by themselves. She began to think there must be an unknown element in pitchblende that made it so radioactive.

Inside the Curie laboratory

A NEW ELEMENT

Finding a new element would be a great discovery. Still, Marie had to prove that such an element existed. She had to find it and separate it from other elements before she could show it to the world. But first she had many hours of difficult work ahead of her. She had to get her hands on piles and piles of pitchblende, and she would need a variety of materials for all the tests she had to run on it. She also needed a place to work.

Pierre helped her find a shed that no one was using behind the Sorbonne's School of Physics and Chemistry. It was damp and cold and had a dirt floor, but it was the best place Marie could get. She immediately went to work. She put her pitchblende in huge pots and then she cooked it and stirred it and ground it into powder. She

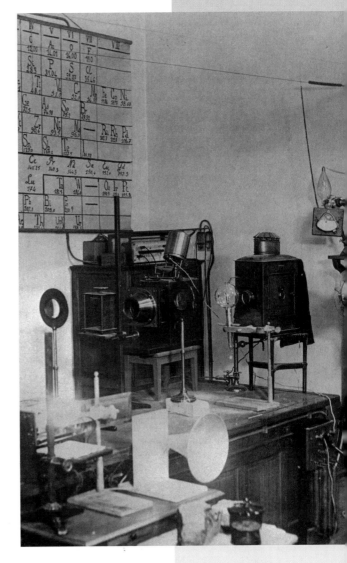

added chemicals to it. She was trying to separate all the elements that made up pitchblende. Sometimes, she and Pierre would work on experiments together.

At the end of her day, Marie's arms ached from all the lifting and stirring. She was tired from trying to figure out how to find the new element, but every day she returned to the shed for more experiments. Finally, after months of work, she and Pierre found what they were looking for. It was a new element, and it was four hundred times more radioactive than any other element. Pierre and Marie named it **polonium** in honor of Poland, Marie's native land.

DISCOVERING RADIUM

Not long after this, the Curies discovered another new element, which they called **radium**. Its name came from the Latin word for "ray." Radium was even more radioactive than polonium. Marie and Pierre had been working for four years to separate radium from other elements, and now the Curies were finally able to see the new element they had discovered. It gave off a silvery glow. They stood together in the shed and looked at the glowing radium. Years later, Marie remembered that it looked like magic.

The Pleasures of Science

Later in her life, Marie remembered her feelings about the Curie laboratory:

*One of our pleasures was to enter our workshop at night. Then, all around us, we would see the **luminous** silhouettes of the beakers and capsules that contained our products.*

Pierre and Marie Curie were dedicated to their work.

CHAPTER 6

FINDING FAME

Wile Marie and Pierre were doing their important work, they were also raising their first child. As Marie worked to discover polonium and radium, she also took care of Irène. After a hard day in the shed, she came home to care for the baby.

Marie somehow made time to write down all the details of Irène's growth. As a young mother, she kept a notebook for recording Irène's height, weight, and other important facts. It was just like the notebook she kept for her science experiments, but this one was devoted entirely to Irène.

The Curies' work led to remarkable discoveries and many awards.

A SPECIAL AWARD

In 1903, Marie received her doctorate degree in physics. It was the first degree of its kind awarded to a woman in France, but an even greater honor was on its way.

In November of that same year, the Curies received a message from Sweden. They had been awarded the Nobel Prize in physics. It was the greatest honor a scientist could win, and Marie was the first woman to win it. For their discovery of radioactivity, the Curies shared the Nobel Prize with Antoine Henri Becquerel.

Letters came from all over the world offering congratulations, and reporters flocked to interview the Curies. Other scientists came to hear them speak. They were invited to travel to Sweden to receive the Nobel Prize and to attend grand dinners and glittering ceremonies.

The Nobel Prizes

The Nobel Prizes were created by a Swedish inventor named Alfred Nobel (above). Starting in 1901, five medals were awarded each year: the Nobel Peace Prize and prizes in physics, chemistry, medicine, and literature. In 1969, a prize in economics was added.

ILLNESS

But there was one enormous problem. The Curies were unable to go to Sweden because they were ill. Both of them suffered from what came to be called radiation sickness. They both had severe burns on their hands and became tired very quickly. Marie coughed until she could barely breathe, and she lost weight. All of this was the result of handling radioactive material. At that time, scientists didn't know how dangerous radioactivity

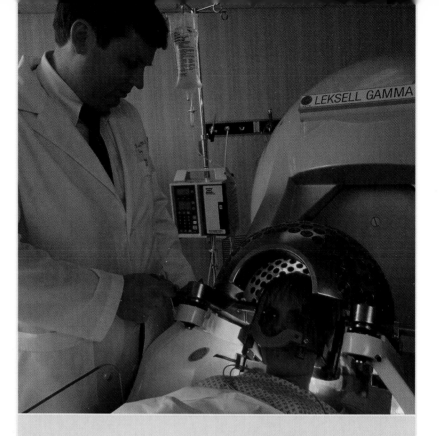

Radiation Sickness

The human body absorbs radiation. Radiation can then cause changes in the cells inside the human body. These changes can lead to diseases such as cancer or leukemia. However, radiation can also be beneficial. Doctors use radiation to help cure sick people (above). They aim radiation only at diseased cells inside the body, so that it will destroy them and leave healthy cells alone.

could be. The Curies had been working with radioactive material every day for years, and they were beginning to feel its effects.

Besides being ill, the Curies were still very poor. They had to work at several jobs to earn enough money to pay the rent. They were more interested in working to earn extra money than in attending fancy parties, so they asked a French official in Stockholm to accept the Nobel Prize for them.

NEW JOBS AND
A NEW DAUGHTER

The Nobel Prize did make life somewhat better for the Curies, however. Pierre was given a good job as a professor at the Sorbonne, and Marie got a job teaching at a women's college. (The Sorbonne was not ready for female professors— yet.) Also, the Nobel Prize brought them a great deal of money. Marie used some of the money to help poor students from Poland.

In 1904, Marie gave birth to Eve, her second daughter. Around the same time, the Sorbonne gave Pierre and Marie a new laboratory to work in, which was a great improvement on the old shed. They even found time to take a few vacations in the country. They had no way of knowing that disaster would soon strike.

Marie Curie with her daughter Eve in 1908

CHAPTER 7

WORK AND LOSS

Pierre Curie's life came to an end on a busy Paris street.

The morning of Thursday, April 19, 1906, started like every other morning for the Curies. As Marie cared for their two daughters, Pierre Curie called good-bye to them and left for work. Later that day, while walking through Paris, Pierre stepped into the street without

looking. Had he looked, he would have seen a horse-drawn delivery wagon headed straight at him. The driver of the wagon yelled a warning at Pierre and tried to stop, but it was too late. The wagon struck Pierre, killing him instantly.

CARRYING ON

Marie was devastated by her husband's death. They had shared everything. They had worked together and traveled together and raised their family together. Now Marie was left to care for her two daughters on her own. She began wearing only black, as a symbol of her great sadness. Her friends said she seemed like a different person without Pierre.

Still, someone would have to continue Pierre's research in the laboratory and carry on his work. Someone would have to teach his classes at the Sorbonne too. Marie could do all these things, and it was appropriate that she carry on her husband's work, but officials at the Sorbonne did not offer her Pierre's job right away. She was a woman, after all, and the Sorbonne had no female professors. Finally, the school's officials realized that

After losing her husband, Marie struggled to continue as a scientist and a mother.

Marie was the only person who could possibly take Pierre's place, so she became the first woman to teach at the Sorbonne. One Monday morning she walked into a lecture hall at the Sorbonne, faced the rows and rows of students who filled the seats, and began teaching the class. Marie picked up right where Pierre had left off.

A SECOND NOBEL PRIZE

In 1911, Marie was awarded the Nobel Prize for chemistry, becoming the first person to win two Nobel Prizes. This time, she went to Sweden to accept the award, which was given for her work with radium.

Curie and Einstein

On a vacation with her daughters, Marie met the great scientist Albert Einstein (right), and they became close friends. They enjoyed hiking in the mountains together, and Einstein liked to tell Marie silly jokes. Einstein said of her, "Marie Curie is, of all celebrated beings, the one whom fame has not corrupted."

Not long after she returned to Paris, Marie Curie collapsed and had to be rushed to the hospital. Again she faced the health problems that resulted from her exposure to radioactivity. Though she remained ill through much of 1912 and 1913, she tried to continue working. She helped plan the French Radium Institute in Paris and became its director. The institute was devoted to finding uses for radium, and top scientists from all over the world came there to work.

During World War I (1914–1918), there was even more urgent work for Marie. Doctors used X-ray equipment to treat wounded soldiers in hospitals, but Marie

Soldiers in World War I being diagnosed by a portable X-ray machine

Protecting Radium

The French Radium Institute (left) kept a small supply of radium to use for research. When German troops began marching toward Paris during World War I, Marie worried that France would lose its valuable radium. She put the radium in a lead case (radium would not penetrate lead) and boarded a train. She carried the radium to another city, until it was safe to return it to Paris.

wanted to find a way to treat the wounded on the front lines—before it was too late. Marie soon developed a small X-ray machine that could be moved from place to place. Then she began turning ordinary cars into mobile X-ray units that could follow the troops wherever they went. She even learned to drive and take care of the cars.

TRAVELS

After the war, Marie tried to raise funds for the French Radium Institute. By now, scientists were beginning to understand radium's dangers. They used lead screens to protect themselves from radioactivity, and they did not touch radium with their bare hands. They also learned that radium had beneficial effects, and they experimented with using it to treat a wide range of illnesses. Researchers at the institute needed radium for their work, but because it was so hard to separate from other elements, pure radium was very expensive.

In 1921, Marie went to the United States to raise money to buy radium. She talked with students at

Marie Curie with
President Harding in 1921

The Radium Craze

In the years following the discovery of radium, people were excited about its powers. Because it produced a blue glow, watchmakers began painting radium on watch faces, unaware of how harmful radium could be. Workers at a watch factory in the United States became very ill after working with radium every day. Their teeth began falling out, and their bones began to weaken. All the sick workers died within ten years. Their tragic deaths made more people aware of radium's dangers, and those who worked with radium learned to protect themselves against it and use it wisely.

women's colleges and gave speeches to hundreds of groups all over the country. President Warren Harding gave Marie a gift—a gram of radium. Even such a small bit of radium cost thousands of dollars.

ENDINGS

In 1932, Marie Curie helped open a new Radium Institute in her hometown of Warsaw. (Poland had regained its independence when World War I ended in 1918.) She led the

Irène Curie and her
husband, Frédéric Joliot,
in their laboratory

Marie Curie (second
from right) attending the
opening of the Radium
Institute in Warsaw

way in setting rules for measuring quantities of radium, and she worked tirelessly to stockpile it so that research into its uses could continue.

All of these efforts helped the scientists who would follow in her footsteps. One of those scientists was her daughter Irène, who became a chemist. Marie's other daughter, Eve, also enjoyed success of her own. She went on to become a musician and playwright.

After years of working long hours and handling dangerous materials, Marie's illness finally caught up with her. She became sick with leukemia, an often deadly disease, caused by her exposure to radiation. On July 4, 1934, Marie Curie died.

Marie's important work continued, however. She had started writing a book about radioactivity before she died, and it was published one year after her death. Her daughter Eve wrote a biography of her mother that helped bring Marie Curie's story to thousands of readers.

Marie's other daughter honored her mother in her own way. Like her mother, Irène Curie went on to do research in radioactivity. And, like her mother, she won a Nobel Prize for her work. She shared the 1935 prize for chemistry with her husband, Frédéric Joliot.

The inscription on the Panthéon, a memorial in Paris where many famous people are buried, reads: "To the fatherland's great men, in gratitude." Among those who have been laid to rest there are author Victor Hugo, politician Jean Jaurès, and World War II Resistance fighter Jean Moulin. On April 21, 1995, Maria Curie's ashes were enshrined under the famous dome of the Panthéon, and she became the first woman to receive this honor for her own achievements. (The Panthéon already contained the ashes of one woman, but only as the wife of the chemist and politician Marcellin Berthelot.) This honor recognizes her remarkable accomplishments and pays tribute to her determination and spirit.

Eve Curie went on to be a musician and playwright.

TIMELINE

1867	Marie Curie is born Maria Sklodowska on November 7 in Warsaw, Poland
1877	Her mother dies, and the family home becomes a boardinghouse
1883	Graduates from high school
1891	Moves to Paris to study at the Sorbonne
1893	Becomes the first woman to earn a physics degree from the Sorbonne
1895	Marries Pierre Curie in a simple wedding ceremony
1897	Gives birth to first daughter, Irène; begins her work on radioactivity
1898	Announces discovery of radium and polonium
1903	Shares the Nobel Prize in physics with Pierre Curie and Antoine Henri Becquerel
1904	Gives birth to second daughter, Eve
1906	Pierre Curie dies
1911	Wins second Nobel Prize, this time in chemistry
1914	Provides mobile X-ray service for wounded soldiers in World War I; helps found the Radium Institute in Paris
1921	Tours the United States
1932	Helps open the Radium Institute in Warsaw
1934	Dies on July 4

boarders: people who pay for a room to live in and meals at someone's house

chemistry: a science that studies the composition and properties of substances

Crookes tube: an empty glass tube through which an electric current is passed

elements: substances that can't be broken down into other materials

eminent: highly respected and well-known

estate: a large house on a big piece of land, usually in the country

governess: a woman who cares for a child or children in a private household

headmistress: a woman in charge of a school, usually a private boarding school

luminous: glowing

meager: a small amount, not enough

Nobel Prizes: six awards given annually for peace, physics, economics, literature, medicine, and chemistry; begun by Swedish inventor Alfred Nobel

perseverance: the ability to keep trying even though faced with many obstacles

physics: a science that studies natural laws

pitchblende: a dark-brown or black mineral that contains radium

polonium: a radioactive metallic element

radioactivity: the giving off of energetic and often harmful rays by certain elements

radium: a brilliant white radioactive metallic element, which can be harmful but is also used in the treatment of cancer

Sorbonne: the school of theology at the University of Paris; sometimes the university itself is referred to as the Sorbonne as well

theology: the study of religion

X rays: electromagnetic radiations that can pass through solid materials

TO FIND OUT MORE

BOOKS

Birch, Beverley, and Christian Birmingham (illustrator). *Marie Curie's Search for Radium.* Hauppauge, N.Y.: Barron's Educational Series, 1996.

Ganeri, Anita. *Marie Curie.* Mankato, Minn.: Thameside Press, 2000.

Parker, Steve. *Marie Curie and Radium.* Broomall, Penn.: Chelsea House, 1995.

Pasachoff, Naomi. *Marie Curie and the Science of Radioactivity.* New York: Oxford University Press, 1996.

Poynter, Margaret. *Marie Curie: Discoverer of Radium.* Springfield, N.J.: Enslow Publishers, 2001.

Strathern, Paul. *Curie and Radioactivity.* New York: Anchor Books, 1999.

INTERNET SITES

American Institute of Physics
http://www.aip.org/history/curie/contents.htm
A detailed biography of the life of Marie Curie beginning with her childhood in Poland.

Female Nobel Prize Laureates
http://www.nobelprizes.com/nobel/women.html
Contains information on Marie Curie and other women who have been Nobel Prize winners.

Marie Curie
http://www.galegroup.com/freresrc/womenhst/curie.htm
A biography of Marie Curie.

Marie and Pierre Curie
http://www.pbs.org/wnet/hawking/cosmostar/html/cstars_curies.html
A brief summary of the work of Marie and Pierre Curie.

Marie Curie–Super Scientist Biography
http://www.energy.ca.gov/education/scientists/curie.html
A brief biography of Marie Sklodowska Curie as well as biographies of other scientists who were pioneers in the field of energy.

Page numbers in *italics*
indicate illustrations.

Becquerel, Antoine Henri, 25,
   25, 31
Berthelot, Marcellin, 43
bicycles, 20, *20*, 21
"boneshaker," 20

cancer, 5, 32
chemistry, 5
Curie, Eve (daughter), 33, *33*, 35,
   43, *43*
Curie, Irène (daughter), 4, 21,
   21, 30, 35, 41, *41*, *42*, 43
Curie, Marie, *4, 5, 7, 11, 13, 17, 19,*
   21, 26, 29, 30, 35, 39, 42
   childhood of, 7–8
   death of, 43
   education of, 4, 7–8, 10–12, 13,
      14, 17–18, 31
   family of, 6, 7–8, *7*
   health of, 31–32, 37, 43
   marriage of, 19, 21
   motherhood of, 30
Curie, Pierre, 19, *19*, 21, *21*,
   28, *28–29*, 30, *30*, 33, 34–35

Eiffel, Gustave, 15
Eiffel Tower, 15, *15*
Einstein, Albert, 36, *36*
elements, 26

France, 12, 13, 14, 15, *15*, *16*,
   17, 34–35, *34*, 37, 38
"free universities," 10
French language, 17
French Radium Institute, 37, 38, *38*

Harding, Warren G., *39*, 40
Hugo, Victor, 43

Joliot, Frédéric, *41*, 43
Juarës, Jean, 43

laboratory, 5, *5*, *26*, 27, *27*, *28–29*,
   29, 35, *35*
leukemia, 32, 43

mathematics, 11–12, 18
Michaux, Ernest, 20
Michaux, Pierre, 20
Moulin, Jean, 43

Nobel, Alfred, 31, *31*
Nobel Prizes, 5, 31, 32, 36, 43

Panthéon memorial, 43
Paris, France, 12, 13, 14, 15, *15*, *16*,
   17, 34–35, *34*, 38
physics, 4, 5, 12, 18, 31
pitchblende, 27–28
Poland, 6, *6*, 9, *9*, 10, 14, 28, 33, 40
Polish language, 10
polonium, 28, 30

radiation sickness, 31–32
radioactivity, 25, 27, 28, 31–32, *32*,
   37, 43
radium, 28, 30, 36, 37, 38, 40, 43
Radium Institute (Poland), 40, *40–41*
Robert of Sorbon, 14
Roentgen, Wilhelm, 22, *22*, 23, 24
Russia, 9, 10
Russian language, 10

Sklodowska, Bronya (sister), 11,
   11, 18
Sklodowska family, 6–8, *7*
Sklodowska, Maria. *See* Curie,
   Marie.
Sorbonne, 13, 14,
   14, 18, 27, 33, 35–36

University of Paris, 14, *14*
University of Warsaw, 10

"wandering universities." *See*
   "free universities."
Warsaw, Poland, 6, *6*, 9
World War I, 37–38, *37*, 40

X rays, *22*, 23, *23*, 24–25, *24*, 37,
   37, 38

Zorawski family, 11, 12
Zorawski, Kazimierz, 12

About the Author

Andrew Santella graduated from Loyola University in Chicago and now lives in that city. He writes regularly for a wide range of periodicals, including the *New York Times Book Review* and *Gentlemen's Quarterly*. He is also the author of a number of nonfiction books for young people.